Not on Your Life

Peter Leigh

Published in association with
The Basic Skills Agency

Hodder

A MEMBER OF TH

Acknowledgements
Illustrations: Juan Hayward.
Cover: Juan Hayward.

Orders: please contact Bookpoint Ltd, 130 Milton Park, Abingdon, Oxon OX14 4SB. Telephone: (44) 01235 827720, Fax: (44) 01235 400454. Lines are open from 9.00-6.00, Monday to Saturday, with a 24 hour message answering service. You can also order through our website at www.hodderheadline.co.uk

British Library Cataloguing in Publication Data
A catalogue record for this title is available from The British Library

ISBN 0 340 72090 5

First published 1998
Impression number   10 9 8 7 6 5
Year   2006 2005 2004

Copyright © 1998 Peter Leigh.

Typeset by Fakenham Photosetting Ltd, Fakenham, Norfolk.
Printed in Great Britain for Hodder & Stoughton Educational, a division of Hodder Headline, 338 Euston Road, London NW1 3BH by Athenaeum Press Ltd, Gateshead, Tyne & Wear.

Not on Your Life

Contents

1	The Paper Shop	1
2	The Challenge	5
3	The House	17
4	Back at the Shop	27

1

The Paper Shop

Me, I don't believe in anything!

I don't believe in ghosts.
I don't believe in aliens.
I don't believe in UFOs.
I don't believe in Yetis,
and I don't believe in Santa Claus!

Not on your life!

Kevin and I work as paperboys
at Mr Payne's shop.
Every morning we wait outside
to get the papers.
Kevin and I are always
having these arguments.

He would see something in the paper and say:
'Hey, Curtis! Did you see this?
Aliens have landed in Africa.
Here's a picture of them.'

And he'd show me a picture
of these little green men.

And I'd say:
'That's rubbish. It's fake.
Why do aliens always look like humans
except with bigger eyes?
Why don't they look like birds,
or fish or something?'

And Kevin would say:
'If they looked like you,
they wouldn't look like human beings.'

And then one evening, he said:
'Did you know they've invented time travel?
They're keeping it quiet,
because it's very expensive.
But soon it'll be cheaper,
and anyone will be able to do it.
I want to go back to cavemen times,
so I can run about with those cavegirls
with no clothes on.'

I just said:
'There can never be time travel.
Not on your life!'

'Why not? You don't know.
You're not a scientist!
Even if they haven't invented it yet,
they could do in the future.'

'Think about it – it's obvious.
Look, if someone invented time travel
in the future, we would know about it.'

'Oh yeah, how?' asked Kevin.

'They would come back and visit us,
and tell us how it worked.
Then we would have time travel.
Or they would go back to the Normans,
or the Romans, or whatever, and tell them,
and they would have time travel.
Once you invent time travel,
you've got rid of time –
there isn't any different time any more,
it's all the same.
And seeing as there still is time –
we get up, deliver the papers, go to school,
come back, deliver more papers,
go home, go to bed, get up,
deliver the papers and so on, and so on –
then clearly there can't be any time travel.'

'You'll need time travel,
if you don't get a move on,'
said old Payne as he gave us our papers.
'I want these shifted fast!'

2

The Challenge

One evening as it was getting colder,
and the nights were drawing in,
Kevin was saying how he didn't like
delivering the papers in the dark,
because a ghost might get him.

'There's lots of spooky bits
on my round,' he said.
'There's long drives with big trees –
a ghost could jump out and get you,
and no-one would ever know.'

'Don't be stupid,' I said.
'There's no such thing as ghosts.
Only fools believe in ghosts.'

'My brother's seen a ghost.'
'Your brother?'
'Yes. Well . . . he met this man who had.'

The others joined in now.
'My dad stayed in a haunted house.'
'Did he see anything?'
'No, but someone else did.'
'My cousin said he knew someone
who had seen a ghost.'

'You see,' I said.
'There's no-one here who
has actually seen a ghost.
There never is –
it's always someone else –
a neighbour, a cousin or a friend.
No-one has ever
seen a ghost themselves!'

'I have,' said a voice.
Everyone turned around.
It was Laura.
She was a quiet kid,
who didn't speak much.

'I have,' she said again,
'I've seen a ghost.'
'Oh yes?' I said sarcastically,
'And when did you see this ghost?'
'Yesterday!' said Laura.
'*Yesterday*? Where?'
'On my round,
at number 43 North Street.'
'Number 43 North Street?' I asked.

'Yes, you know. It's a big old house
in the middle of the estate there.
It was there before the other houses
were built.
You can't see it from the road,
because it's got this big overgrown
garden all around it.

It's nearly falling down now,
and nobody has lived there for years,
because it's haunted.'
'Haunted by who?' asked Kevin.

'The man who lived there –
a man called Joseph Smith,
and his wife and their little daughter.
They all died from some
horrible disease, and ever since,
they have haunted the house.'

'Says who?' I asked.
'Says everybody.'
'Oh yes! Oh yes!
Everybody *says* so, they all *say* so.
But nobody has ever *seen* anything.'

'Yes they have,' said Laura,
'like I said, I've seen them.'

Everyone crowded round.
This was really interesting.

'Go on Laura ... tell us ...
what happened?'

'I was delivering a paper
to this old lady who lives next door.
She was out in the front garden
and she was very upset.
She said her cat was missing,
and she thought it was in number 43.
She wanted me to go in and check.'

'Why didn't she go herself?'

'She was too scared of the ghosts –
everyone down that street
believes in them,
and lots of people have seen them.
But she said that if I went
and the ghosts came,
I could run away quicker
than she could.'

'So did you?' asked Kevin.

'Yes! I was like Curtis.
I didn't believe in ghosts.
Besides, she said she would
give me some money.'

'So what happened?'

'Well, I had to get in first.
That was the biggest problem.
There was this really thick hedge
all around the house.

I found a little gap big enough
for a cat and I had to get right down
and crawl through it.
Even when I got to the other side
it was still like a jungle.
I had to fight my way right through it.
It seemed like I was struggling for ages,
when all of sudden, I came out from
under a bush, and there was the house
right in front of me.'

'Then what happened?' asked Kevin.

'It was all big and black and
run-down. It was really spooky,
even if you don't believe in ghosts.
I was dead scared, and then I heard
this howling coming from inside.
That was enough, I can tell you.
I just wanted out of there!
But then I thought, "that must
be the cat!"

When I listened more closely,
it did sound like a cat.
So I breathed again, and went
up the steps to the front door.'

'God, I would have run away
while I still could,' said Kevin.
'What happened then?'

'There was a window at the side,
and I rubbed away the dirt
and looked in, and there was the cat,
sitting in the middle of the hall.
So I started looking around,
and that's when I saw them.'

'The ghosts?' I asked.

'Yes! It was really dark in there,
and I was trying to see,
when suddenly there were
these three faces – a man, a woman
and a little girl, all ill-looking,
and all staring at me.'

'What did you do?' I asked.
'What would you do?
I just turned and ran.'

'What happened to the cat?'
'It turned up again this morning.
It must have found its way out.'

Everyone was quiet for a moment,
while they took this in.
Then Kevin said to me:
'What do you think about that
then, Curtis?'

I chose my words carefully.
'Rubbish!' I said.
'It's all rubbish.
I don't believe a word of it.'

That really set them going.
Everyone was shouting and arguing.
Laura was saying:
'It's true, I tell you!'

Finally Kevin turned to me and said:
'All right!
You say it's all rubbish – prove it!'

'How can I do that?' I replied.
'By going into this house yourself,
to prove you're not scared.'

The others joined in:
'Go on Curtis, prove it!'

What could I say?
'All right then – when?'
'Now,' said Kevin,
'as soon as we've finished
delivering the papers.'
'Yes now!' shouted everyone.

'But it'll be dark by then,' I said.
'No it won't, not if we're quick.
Besides, what difference
will the dark make?
You don't believe in ghosts.'

'No-o – It's just …'
'What? You're not scared are you?'

'Not on your life!
It's just that it's difficult to see.
That's all.'

'I think you're just trying
to chicken out of it,' said Kevin.

He started making clucking noises:
'Chick … chick … chick … chicken!
Cluck-cluck! Cluck-cluck!'

'All right! I'll do it,' I said.

Everyone cheered,
and just at that moment,
old Payne came out with the papers.

'What's all the noise?' he asked.
'Curtis is going
to the haunted house – *tonight*!'

3

The House

Like I said, I don't believe
in anything, especially not ghosts.
But there's something about going
into an old, empty house,
when it's just beginning to get dark,
that would make anyone nervous.

Which is why I wasn't feeling
too good as I finished my round.

I hitched my bag over my shoulder –
there were a few papers left –
and turned towards North Street.

There was a crowd of kids
already there.
Kevin must have told everybody.
They gave a cheer as I rode up.
Kevin was at the centre
of the crowd with Laura.

'All right,' I said.
'What do you want me to do?'

Kevin spoke loudly and clearly,
as if he wanted everyone to hear.
'You have to go through the garden,
go right into the house,
and fetch something back,
to prove you've been there.'

'OK then! No problem!' I was
sounding a lot better than I felt.
'How do I get in?'

'Show him, Laura,' said Kevin.
Laura pulled back the hedge,
and there was a gap at the bottom.
'Through there!'

'Right then, off I go,' I said.
'By the way,' said Kevin,
'If you're not back in half an hour,
we'll phone the police.'

'Thanks a lot, Kev,' I said,
feeling worse than ever.

I got down on my hands and knees,
and began to crawl forwards.
I had to go right down on my stomach
to get through the hedge.

Laura was right,
it was like a jungle in there.
After a few yards, it was silent –
I couldn't hear anything
from the street.

I managed to get on my feet
when I got past the hedge,
but it was still really thick.

I blundered about for a bit,
not really sure where I was going,
and then suddenly, just like Laura
had said, I came out from a bush,
and there was a house
right in front of me.

It certainly was a spooky place.
It was all dark and boarded-up.
There was a big old porch,
full of dead leaves and cobwebs.
I pushed them aside,
and went up to the front door.
I could see the window on one side,
and the little patch that Laura
had wiped clean.

I went over to it, bent down,
and peered through.

The first thing I saw was
Joseph Smith staring back at me,
together with his wife and daughter.
I didn't scream or run or anything,
because to tell the truth,
I was half-expecting it.

I just carried on looking,
until my eyes got used to the dark.

I soon saw what I was looking for –
the shape of a picture frame
around Joseph Smith.
I smiled to myself.
I had thought it must be a picture
as Laura was telling the story.

I went back to the front door.
It was still very stiff,
but I managed to push it open
a few inches, just enough
for me to squeeze through the crack.
Everything was thick with dust.
Nobody had been there for years.

I went to look at the pictures.
I could see why Laura
had thought they looked ill.
They were so covered with dust
they were all grey-looking.
They were weird pictures though.
The eyes seemed to stare at you
wherever you were in the room.

Joseph Smith looked very stern,
and so did Mrs Smith.
She looked cruel too.
The daughter was smiling at me.
But it wasn't a nice smile at all.
It was the sort of smile you see
on a cat's face just after it has
caught a bird.

The three pictures were all
in a line facing the door,
and there was a much smaller
picture next to them.

I went to have a look at it,
and that was when I nearly died.
The fourth picture was me!

My heart seemed to stop,
my feet seemed stuck to the floor,
and then I breathed again.
'It's a mirror you fool,' I said
to myself, and I took a closer look.

It was a small mirror, just what
I needed as proof that I had been there.
I still had my papers bag
over my shoulder. I lifted it off,
and lay it on the floor.
Then I reached up and tried to
take the mirror off the wall.

This would show I wasn't a chicken,
and there is no such thing as ghosts.
I put the mirror under my jacket,
and made my way back through
the garden.
It seemed much easier on the way
back, even if it was much darker.
It wasn't long before I was back
standing in front of the others.

'I've done it,' I said. 'I've been
in the house, and there's no such
thing as ghosts. And to prove it,
here is the mirror from the hall.'
I held it up like at the Cup Final.

Then I told them about the pictures,
and how scary they were,
and how people could have thought
there were ghosts there.

Everyone started patting me
on the back.
'Well done Curtis,' they said.

Suddenly I remembered the papers bag.
I had left it in the hall
when I picked up the mirror.
'Oh God!' I said,
and told Kevin what I had done.
'Old Payne will kill you,' he said.

It was now completely dark.
Everything was pitch black.
I wouldn't be able to find
anything in that.

'I'll have to go and tell him,'
I said, 'and get the bag tomorrow.'

4

Back at the Shop

I rode back to the shop,
feeling really down.
This was not going to be easy.
Old Payne was always looking for
an excuse to sack someone.

The bell tinkled as I opened the door,
and old Payne looked up and saw me.

'Mr Payne,' I said, 'I'm sorry ...'
'Sorry? I should think you are!
You're a thief,
and you're giving me a bad name.'

Thief? What did he mean?
'Mr Payne, I'm sorry, but ...'

'Some man rang from number 43
North Street. He had a strange,
far away sounding voice. He said
something about a stolen mirror.
He mentioned your name,
then the phone went dead.
Do you know anything
about it Curtis?'

That was yesterday. Like I said,
I don't believe in ghosts.
I know there's an explanation.
But have I been back
to number 43 North Street?
Not on your life!